TIME CAPSULE

A book filled with creative drawing and writing prompts

Laura van Barneveld

First Edition, 2016

For more information go to:

www.lauravanbarneveld.com

Need inspiration?

Watch me filling up my Time Capsule on Youtube! Simply type in my full name or use the link below. Take a look at Time Capsule's book page on Facebook and Instagram for pictures of completed pages by me and others. You can also follow me on Instagram and Tumblr for daily creative content.

https://www.youtube.com/user/Yukaa63
https://www.facebook.com/timecapsulebook
@time_capsule (Instagram)
@creativebrainwash (Instagram, Tumblr)

WELCOME

This book is an empty time capsule, waiting to be filled by you! The purpose of this book is to spark the creativity in you and capture a picture of who you are right at this moment. There is so much to discover in this book but at the same time this is a blank canvas to create everything that you desire.

▬ ▬ ▬ ▬ ▬ ▬ ▬ ▬ ▬

Time capsules have always been truly fascinating to me. You bury something in the ground, or put something away for years, just to dig it up in the future and be amazed at what things were popular back then. I always imagined digging up a time capsule would feel like looking at a picture of yourself when you were younger, or seeing a drawing or some writing that you did ages ago. You feel embarrassed but also proud of who you are, were and of the things you accomplished.

The reason I spent a gazillion hours to put this book together is because I wanted something personal. I wanted to create a book that had my vision. Art is very fascinating and great and wonderful, but if there is not a piece of yourself in it, it isn't what it could be. Being the kind of person that I am, I went overboard and went from 'just creating a fun little journal with self thought of prompts for myself' to 'hey look, this is the book I published.' However, I am very glad that I did and that I can share my hard work with everyone.

Time Capsule's uniqueness lies in the personal nature of the prompts. That was the concept of the book from the beginning and I am glad that I was able to turn that vision into something real. Hopefully you enjoy filling up this book with your creations and find out a little bit more about yourself along the way.

Lots of love, Laura

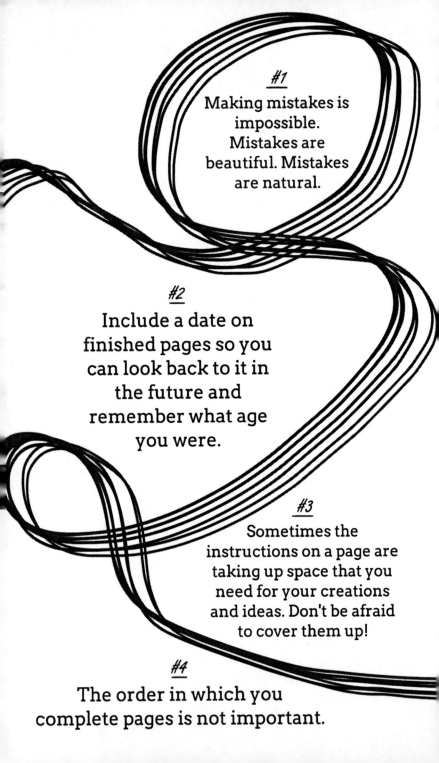

#1

Making mistakes is impossible. Mistakes are beautiful. Mistakes are natural.

#2

Include a date on finished pages so you can look back to it in the future and remember what age you were.

#3

Sometimes the instructions on a page are taking up space that you need for your creations and ideas. Don't be afraid to cover them up!

#4

The order in which you complete pages is not important.

DIRECTIONS

#7

Ignore these directions and do whatever you want. This is YOUR time capsule!

#6

Share your finished pages on social media using #time_capsule

#5

Change a prompt if you don't like it or remove it altogether. This is your book and you don't have to do something you don't want to.

MATERIAL GUIDE

Best art supplies to use:

pencils
crayons
acrylic paint
pens
chalk
charcoal
any dry material

Other materials you can use in this book:

- paper
- plastics
- fabric
- wallpaper samples
- yarn
- glitter
- glue
- any small items
  that can be glued in
- tape
- leaves, grass, and
  flowers
- pictures
- cut outs form magazines,
  books, newspapers etc.

- buttons
- old book pages
- feathers
- candy wrappers
- popsicle sticks
- stamps
- ribbons
- bubble wrap
- cardboard

Anything else that you can think of that fits in this book

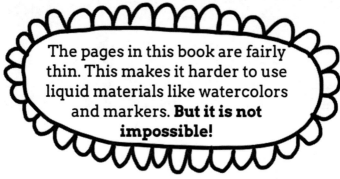

The pages in this book are fairly thin. This makes it harder to use liquid materials like watercolors and markers. **But it is not impossible!**

I recommend two things for covering up bled through materials. One is **sticking a piece of sketch or printer paper over a page**. Simply glue it on and trim it even to the book. You can also use **gesso**, which is a kind of primer. You can paint over the page and the stains will disappear. However, you can't use every material over a gesso layer. Gesso can be bought at most craft stores.

Ignore whatever bled through the page. See it as an **opportunity** rather than an ugly burden. Just acknowledge that it is there and work around it or work with it. Maybe you can even incorporate it into the prompt on the page.

Use **less water** when you use paints, and **press less hard** with markers.

Glue in a piece of sketchbook paper or printer paper **before** you start a page. This way the materials you use won't bleed through to the other side. You can also **draw or paint on a separate piece of paper** and glue it in the book once you finished.

Try out different materials and what effect they have. There are markers out there that barely or don't bleed through.

BASIC INFO

Name Dhwani Panchal.

Age 25

Country USA – INDIA

Started 6/1/2017

Finished _____

- - - - - - - - -

'I promise to fill up this time capsule and put a piece of myself on every page'

Sign here

Your picture goes here

1. She is one crazy girl
   I know.
            — Swati Gaur

   "Happy 25th Dee" ♥

Hardworking

Impatient

Lazy

Talkative

Curious

Design your
dream
house

Draw yourself as...

You are

an animal

+20 years

a monster

Make up your own words and explain them

Decorate the outside of your

Time Capsule

and all pages without a prompt,

including this one

Fill
this
page
with things that feel like *home*

Make a **bucketlist** *for the next* 365 days

06/01/2017 :-

Microsoft, Tesla or any Big company.
   (Silicon Valley)

2. Get super slim

3. Visit Europe

4. Do a course in scuba diving

5. Become champ in coding.

6.

Hopes &
Dreams

Collect receipts
and glue them here

123456789

Document the *sounds* you hear all around you

Practice your handwriting
here

Make this page
Delicious

Fill this page with *childhood memories*

I

AM

Document life

Describe what you see all around you

Create your current family tree

06/01/2017.

Dads. Dad. → Arvind kaka
→ Nami raja
→ Dilipdada bhai
→ anddi

My dady (Dadi) ↓
Nana (Nani)

Achiuwati Dada

(BA)

Ishar kaka (alka kaki)   Mahesh kaka (Bharna kaki)

My dad kaka Chetto   kaka (kaka)   Kod Parosh (vender)   bhavika kaki

Me   kanan   Sneh N.   Josh Man

Kaipil (apana bhai)   kunal (sonal bhabhi)   Kushal

↓ kushin

Aaja (Aaj.)
Mama Mai
Risa Relly

Dada
↓
Fui (Runa Bhavin)

What superhero power would you like to have?

Answer these *or/or questions*

06/17

Fruit *or* Vegetables
Books *or* Magazines
Hoodies *or* Tank tops/t-shirts
Spicy *or* Mild
Mornings *or* Evenings
Fiction *or* Reality
Call *or* Text
Glasses *or* Contacts
Save *or* Spend
Pirates *or* Ninjas
Board games *or* Video games
Hardwood *or* Carpet
Long hair *or* Short hair
Pen *or* Pencil
House *or* Apartment

Headphones *or* Earbuds

Dogs *or* Cats

Paint *or* Colored pencils

Physical book *or* E-book

Laptop *or* Desktop

Sun vacation *or* Sightseeing *or* Adventure

Summer *or* Winter

Instagram *or* Twitter

Movies *or* TV Series

Singing *or* Dancing

Tattoo *or* Piercing

Antique *or* Brand new

Zoo *or* Amusement park

Introvert *or* Extrovert

Black and white *or* Color

Birthday *or* Christmas

Backpack *or* Purse

Doodle on these pages *or* Not

Illustrate a part of your favorite book

What makes you
SCARED?

Make a *list of firsts*

(pet, job, concert, etc.)

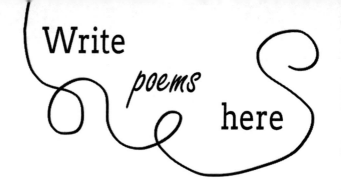
Write *poems* here

create a monster

If you could go *anywhere* right now, where would you go?

Fill this page
with things that
are popular

right now

Make up your own

secret code

Create a map of all the places you have EVER been

Look at the stars

and create your own *constellations*

Stick one or multiple pictures on these pages

and create
frames out of

uncooked pasta

Fill this page with *quotes* and *lyrics*

What **5** things would you grab if your house was

on **FIRE**

Find out **everything** you can about *the day you were born*

Date of birth: _____

Make a list of all your *favorite words*

Turn yourself or someone you know into a **cartoon**

Fill this page when you **can't sleep**

Change the world with this piece of paper

Write a letter to
your future self

List all the things you are *satisfied* with

List all your regrets

Go **crazy** with a
hole puncher

*complete the pages before and after this one first

Complain here

Be positive

Design your dream car

What are your *guilty pleasures?*

Collect
ticket stubs
and glue them here

Write

non-stop

Create a word or drawing for each letter of the alphabet.

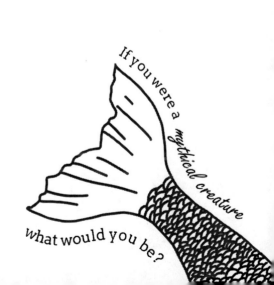

If you were a mythical creature what would you be?

Put your *culture* on this page

Have important
people in your life
sign this page

Describe what you consider to be *perfect weather*

Create an alter ego

I would wake up in the *middle of the night* for...

Dedicate this page to learning something

(school notes, new language, math formulas, how to cook, etc.)

Daydream on this page

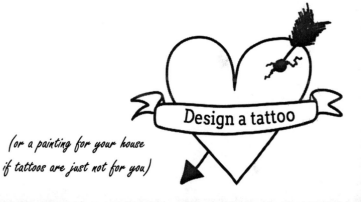

Design a tattoo

(or a painting for your house
if tattoos are just not for you)

This is some space

for when you need it

Create a pocket

to collect small things you find

Write *a story* from a
lifeless object's perspective

Who is your *idol?*

Look at the **clouds** *and document what you see in them*

Write down your *favorite recipe*

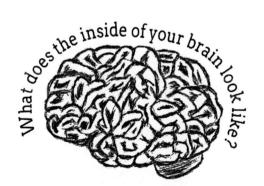

What does the inside of your brain look like?

Make a wish

Draw
people you
know as
animals

Make a list of things

you look forward to

Word game!

Write down the first word that comes to mind when you think of the word written on the right page. Then, write down the first thing that comes to mind when you think of the word you just wrote. Continue until the page is full. Circle the last word. Compare with other people!

Collect sugar packets and napkins from restaurants and glue them down.

write down where you got them

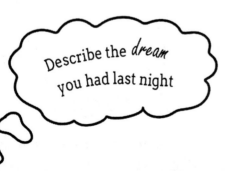

Describe the *dream* you had last night

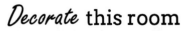

Decorate this room

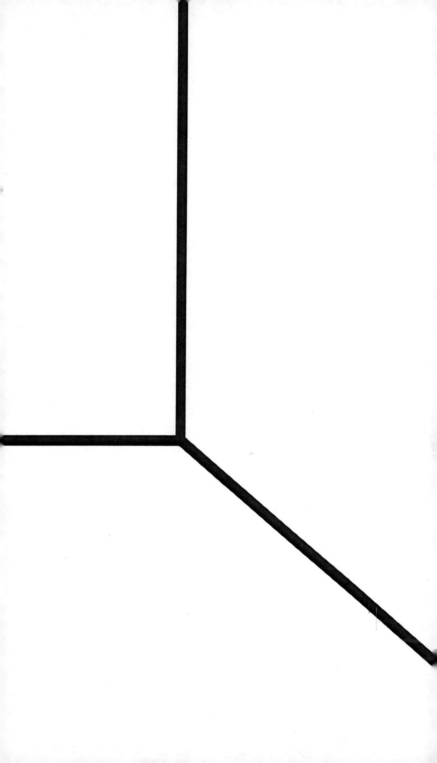

Make a list of all the *professions* you ever considered

Describe your current *mood* and *feelings*

What 3 items would you take to a deserted island?

Thoughts & *ideas*

What do you *truly* believe in?

Doodle

these

Tell an *awkward* (true) story

Invent something

Fill this page

with *recent* newspaper articles

This text is absolutely useless and has no meaning. The picture above is of my dog Teemo. He is really fluffy and awesome! He is really active and will steal your food any chance he gets. I don't really have anything else to say about my dog.

If you are still reading this you should really grab a real newspaper and start cutting out real articles and stop reading this nonsense. I don't even know for how long newspapers will physically exist because we are reaching a point where everyone is able to look it up on the internet. It is a waste of paper, really.

Now I'll just write a little about the apple that is on my desk next to my laptop. It is red and yellow. I don't know if I should eat it. I thought that I would get hungry, but I am still full from lunch. Dinner is going to be in 2 hours. Apples are tasty though. Except for the time I took a bite out of an apple and a bug came crawling out. I didn't know that could actually happen.

One time I tried to put an apple in a smoothie. I make fruit smoothies very often but had never tried apple in it before. Well, it was disgusting. The texture of the smoothie became really... weird. I'll just stick to putting bananas, strawberries and oranges in my smoothies.

Winter is my favorite season but I don't like that it is getting dark so quickly. I have to turn on the lights at 3pm because my house doesn't have many windows. However, I love the cold weather and wearing hoodies and thick wooly socks and sleeping under three blankets.

I didn't know what to write about anymore so I decided to eat my apple anyway. Lately I have been trying to eat better and exercise more. I have tried that a few times before but failed. This time though it is going better. Probably because I am really doing it for myself this time, and for my future.

It is very cold in my room right now and I can't decide if I should just turn up the heater, put on another sweater or get another blanket. My fingers are like icicles so I should probably get some gloves too. I have gloves with the fingertips cut of laying around here somewhere....

Well, I couldn't find them. I grabbed a sweater that is waaaaaaaay too big on me. So the sleeves are kind of functioning as my gloves.

After another hour in my room it really got too cold to function. I didn't want to turn on the heater so I grabbed everything I was using and went downstairs. My fingers are slowly turning warm again and so is my nose. Now I can comfortably finish writing this nonsense story without cold limbs.

By now you should really be bored with my story. I suggest you grab a newspaper or two and start cutting out some articles that spark your interest. You don't have to limit the size of the articles to the space on this page. You can let them stick out and fold it in. Or you could staple some articles together and glue the bottom one down. The possibilities are endless.

For those who never receive any newspapers at home, you can also go online and find articles. You could print them and glue them in. If you really dislike newspapers and want to do something different you could create your own article. About you, your life, school, your family, work or your dog. Whatever you come up with, please cover up this boring story that is not meant for you to read but meant to fill up space and make this page look like a newspaper. But no, you just had to read it, didn't you?

Anyways, we are coming to an end here. Congratulations, you made it to the end. Go get a cookie (and a newspaper) and start working on this page. You better make it prettier than this story. But before you start, you should turn up the music really loud (and sing along) because that makes everything more fun! Well, good luck, may the newspaper be filled with awesome stories.

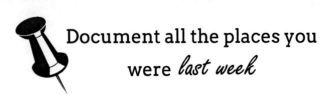

Document all the places you were *last week*

Picture yourself in an outfit
you would normally *never wear*
(you could draw, photograph, collage etc.)

Come up with an *alternate ending* to your favorite tv-series or movie

Make a one-week food diary

What would you never, ever do?

Make up a story about a *stranger* you see somewhere

Design a sightseeing brochure for the place where you live

(country, city, etc.)

List all the things you like about yourself

Make a schedule of a typical day

Take pictures of your surroundings. Glue them down and document where they were taken.

Decorate this page with your favorite holiday or season

Make up your own *joke*

What do you think your life will look like in *15 years?*

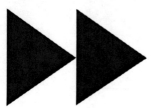

List all the things
you want *to buy*

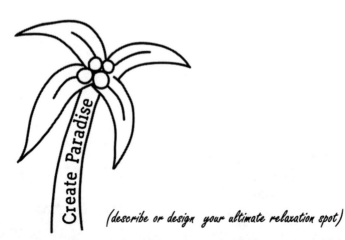

Create Paradise

(describe or design your ultimate relaxation spot)

Make a list of things that make you smile

Fill this page with things you consider to be *Lucky*

Collect notes you have written and glue them here

Rant about the horrible day you had today

List all your *accomplishments* on this page

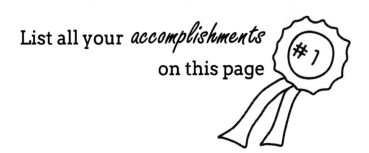

Draw
your
favorite
place
to be

Create a

business

Make a timeline of yourself. Use pictures, drawings, notes or anything else you can think of

If you would
have *one day*
left to live,
how would
you spend it

How to bury a real time capsule:

If you want to bury a time capsule, you need something that can hold everything and is **waterproof**. For example, a mason jar.

Fill it up with **memories** and current things. Pictures, letters, a newspaper, tickets etc. Take a good look around your house for things you can use. If you live with your parents, make sure you have their permission to put the things you chose in your Time Capsule.

Find a spot to bury or keep it. If it is a personal time capsule, consider burying it in your **backyard** or storing it in the **attic**. Do not dig a hole in public or someone else's property without permission!

Make sure you put the **opening date** on the container. You can decide yourself for how long your time capsule will be closed. If you don't want anyone else to open your time capsule, you can write that on the outside.

Don't forget about your time capsule. Put a **reminder** on your phone or computer somewhere. Also, if you buried it in your backyard, don't forget to temporarily dig it up if you move!

How to turn this book into a time capsule:

Put it in a **container**. If you are planning to bury it, it needs to be waterproof. You can also tape it closed or put multiple plastic bags around it before you put it in a container, so that absolutely nothing can harm your book.

If you don't want to bury it, you could close the book (either just close it or really tape/tie/pack it closed) and put it away somewhere. This way you won't have to bury it but you can't look in it either. You could put it on a **shelf in your attic** or **stored in a box**. Make sure that everyone who lives with you knows about this and won't accidentally open it.

Put a **date** on the book or on the container it is in! You can also put the date you buried it or stored it away on the outside.

If you want more tips and tricks for creating a time capsule, there is a lot more information to find on the internet!

Good luck, and have fun!

Do **whatever** you want on this page, as long as this is the very, very, very, last alteration you make to this book

Create a flip-through video of your **Time Capsule** and upload it to youtube

Take pictures of completed pages and post them on *Instagram, Facebook, Tumblr,* or wherever you desire

#time_capsule

I can't wait to see what you have created!

Lots of love,

Laura

CPSIA information can be obtained
at www.ICGtesting.com
Printed in the USA
LVOW11s2106050517
533217LV00001B/13/P

9 781364 516536